Apples

by Ann L. Burckhardt

Reading Consultant:
Julia Daly
International Apple Institute

Bridgestone Books
an Imprint of Capstone Press

Bridgestone Books are published by Capstone Press
818 North Willow Street, Mankato, Minnesota 56001
Copyright © 1996 by Capstone Press
Printed in the United States of America

Library of Congress Cataloging-in-Publication Data
Burckhardt, Ann, 1933-
    Apples/ by Ann L. Burckhardt
    p. cm.--(Early-reader science. Foods.)
    Includes bibliographical references (p.24) and index.
    Summary: Simple text introduces apples, and instructions are given for making an
    apple pomander.
    ISBN 1-56065-448-1
    1.Apples--Juvenile literature. 2. Nature craft--Juvenile literature. [1.Apples.]
    I. Title. II. Series.
SF487.5.B735 1996
636.5--dc20

                                                                    95-54167
                                                                       CIP
                                                                        AC

Photo credits
Unicorn/Martha McBride, cover; Joseph Fontenot, 12; Alice Prescott, 14.
International Stock, 4, 10, 20.
Michelle Coughlan, 6, 16.
FPG, 8.
Corbis-Bettmann, 18.

Table of Contents

Words in **boldface** type in the text are defined in the Words to Know section in the back of this book.

What Are Apples?

Apples are one of the most popular fruits. The world produces more than 2 billion **bushels** of apples every year. The average person eats 50 apples every year.

Different Kinds of Apples

There are more than 7,500 different kinds of apples. Some are grown to be sold in stores. These include McIntosh, Granny Smith, Delicious, Golden Delicious, and Rome.

Parts of an Apple

An apple has five main parts. They are the skin, **flesh**, core, seeds, and stem. The skin of an apple can be red, yellow, or green. The flesh of an apple can taste sweet or **tart**.

Where Apples Grow

Apples grow on an apple tree. They grow best in areas that have cool winters. During the winter, apple trees prepare for growing again. The state of Washington produces the most apples in North America.

How Apples Grow

In the spring, buds appear on apple tree branches. The buds grow leaves and then flowers. When the flowers die, green bulges start growing in their place. These bulges grow into apples.

Harvest

Apples are ready to **harvest** when they can be easily pulled off the tree. Harvesters pick the apples by hand. They use ladders to reach the high branches.

How We Use Apples

Apples are used to make many things. Apple cider, applesauce, and apple butter are made with apples. Eating an apple is very good for your teeth.

History

Pilgrims brought apples to North America. Presidents Washington and Jefferson both grew apple trees. Johnny Appleseed lived in the early 1800s. He walked from farm to farm planting apple seeds for many years.

Apples and People

People say an apple a day keeps the doctor away. They say some things are as American as apple pie. New York City is called the Big Apple.

Hands On: Make an Apple Pomander

A pomander is an air freshener made from fruit and cloves. In the past, pomanders were often used to freshen rooms.

You will need
- a firm apple
- fork
- ground cinnamon
- whole cloves
- bowl
- ribbon
- 8-inch (20-centimeter) square of nylon net

1. Use a fork to prick holes in the apple.
2. Push the stem of a whole clove into each hole.
3. Put the apple in a bowl. Sprinkle ground cinnamon on it.
4. Let the apple and bowl sit in a cool place for a few days.
5. Put the apple in the center of the nylon net.
6. Tie the top of the net with ribbon.
7. Hang or set the pomander in your room. It will smell sweet and fresh.

Words to Know

bushel—dry unit of measure equal to 32 quarts (35 liters), or about 100 apples
flesh—the edible part of a fruit or vegetable
harvest—gather a crop
tart—sharp sour taste

Read More

De Bourgoing, Pascale. *Fruit*. A First Discovery Book. New York: Scholastic, 1991.

Lindbergh, Reeve. *Johnny Appleseed*. Boston: Little, Brown, 1990.

Maestro, Betsy. *How Do Apples Grow?* New York: HarperCollins, 1992.

Micucci, Charles. *The Life and Times of the Apple*. New York: Orchard Books, 1992.

Index

A Seriously Silly Story
of a Waterdrops Journey

Written by Martha Miller

Illustrated by Becca Vaughn

LifeRich Publishing is a registered trademark of The Reader's Digest Association, Inc.

LifeRich Publishing books may be ordered through booksellers or by contacting:

LifeRich Publishing
1663 Liberty Drive
Bloomington, IN 47403
www.liferichpublishing.com
1 (888) 238-8637

Interior Image Credit: Becca Vaughn

ISBN: 978-1-4897-2650-6 (sc)
ISBN: 978-1-4897-2649-0 (e)

Printed in the United States of America.

LifeRich Publishing rev. date: 01/10/2020

A Seriously Silly Story
of a Waterdrops Journey

Hi! My name is Scooter, and I am a water droplet. I've been around for a very long time, which makes me a bazillion years old. But every time I come to visit earth, I feel like a kid again!

I have taken many journeys to earth, and each one is its own adventure!

I've helped big barges float down the Mississippi River. I love it when I get into the animals' water trough. Did you know that cows have four stomachs?

I know; I've been through all four! I got all caught up in a cow once and ended up coming out as *milk!*

Once, while on a journey, I was a hero and helped put out a house fire. I've had a ton of adventures! See, water drops just keep going around and around and around. We never stop— well, except for my cousin Leroy and his buddies that are frozen in those glaciers. They don't move around as much as some of the rest of us drops do.

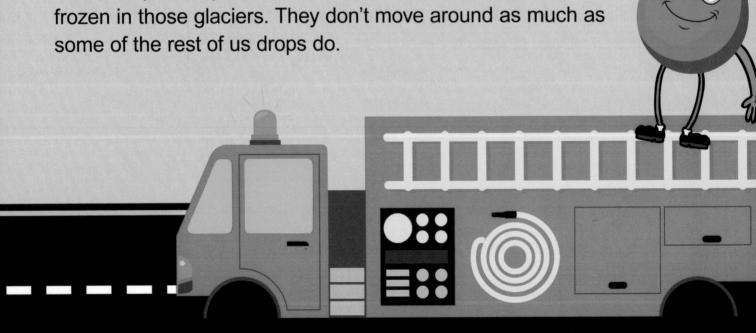

I'm about to leave the clouds for another journey. Hey—would you like to come along with me?

Well, all righty, then. Let's get going.

Falling down from the big clouds is called precipitation.

Precipitating (or falling down) is easy, unless you get into one of those thunderstorms where all the drops fall fast and furiously.

I must say it's not as nice as the time I landed in the middle of that hayfield and sank into the ground to become *groundwater* for a few months. Sometimes waterdrops can stay in the ground for months or even years.

Oh, well … let's see where we go next!

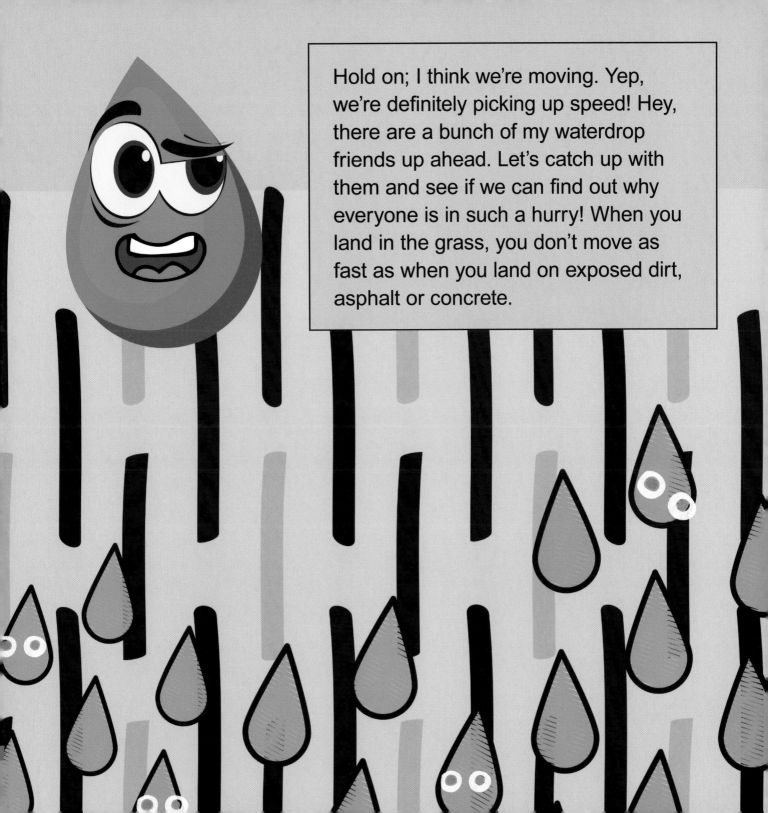

Hold on; I think we're moving. Yep, we're definitely picking up speed! Hey, there are a bunch of my waterdrop friends up ahead. Let's catch up with them and see if we can find out why everyone is in such a hurry! When you land in the grass, you don't move as fast as when you land on exposed dirt, asphalt or concrete.

But why so soon? If we stick around longer, we can do some really great things, like make trees and plants grow big and strong and help animals too! Besides, all of us drops know we can get good and clean if we stick around in healthy soil for a little while. When we all go so quickly, we don't get clean, and some of us get sick; remember?

Welcome to what we water drops call the dungeon.

None of us really likes to take this journey through the big city *storm drain.* It's dark and cold, and it really stinks down here. But it seems that more and more of us are taking this journey these days.

We have to be extra careful on this journey because it's so easy to get sick down here. See, you human folks haven't learned yet that not everything you put into the storm drains is good for us water drops!

Stick close, and hopefully, we won't get hurt.

See that oil over there that some of my waterdrop friends are stuck in? It's bad stuff! Oil is water's enemy; we just don't mix well! Once we run into each other down here, it gets ugly. Oil steals water's oxygen, and then others, like dirt, rocks, and sand, start adding to the problem. There seems to be a lot more of this stuff down here these days. You humans call that dirt and stuff sediment and it is one of the worst things for us waterdrops. After a while, we have so much stuff stuck to us that we just can't move anymore.

And then there are the chemicals. What on earth are you humans thinking? You fertilize your yards, you fertilize your golf courses, you use chemicals to kill weeds and certain plants …

Guess what? If the skull and crossbones is bad for humans, it's just as bad for us water drops!

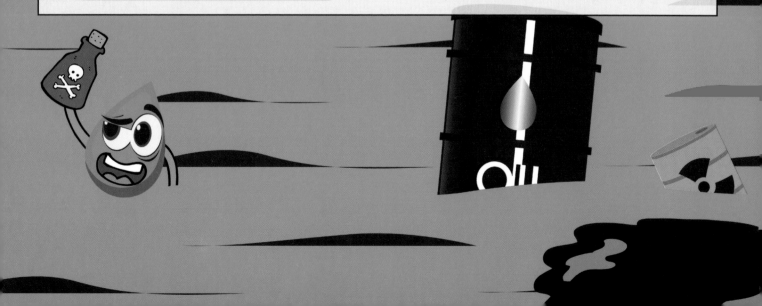

Oh, hey!

Watch out for the empty soda can on your left and the french fry container on your right. We must be getting close to garbage gorge. That's the spot where all the litter and garbage go. When people leave their trash on the road or along sidewalks it often ends up in a storm drain.People don't dump this stuff directly into the streams because they are too busy leaving it on the roads to be washed into the storm drains!

Oh thank goodness, see that light? It's the light at the end of the big city's storm drain system. That means we're about ready to move into a stream, creek, or river.

We'll start to move faster as we near the light or *discharge site*. Like going down the big hill on a roller coaster! Hold on, 'cause *here we go!*.

This is the local creek, so kick back, and enjoy the rest of this journey. In just a few hours, we will be in the local river, and by tomorrow, we will be headed down the Mississippi River toward the Gulf of Mexico!

But before we evaporate back into the air, we water drops affect a lot of things. If we get sick, the things we touch can get sick too — like the farmer's fields where your food is grown …

- the animals that provide milk and food
- plants and animals that make clothes
- trees that provide paper and houses
- and much, much more!

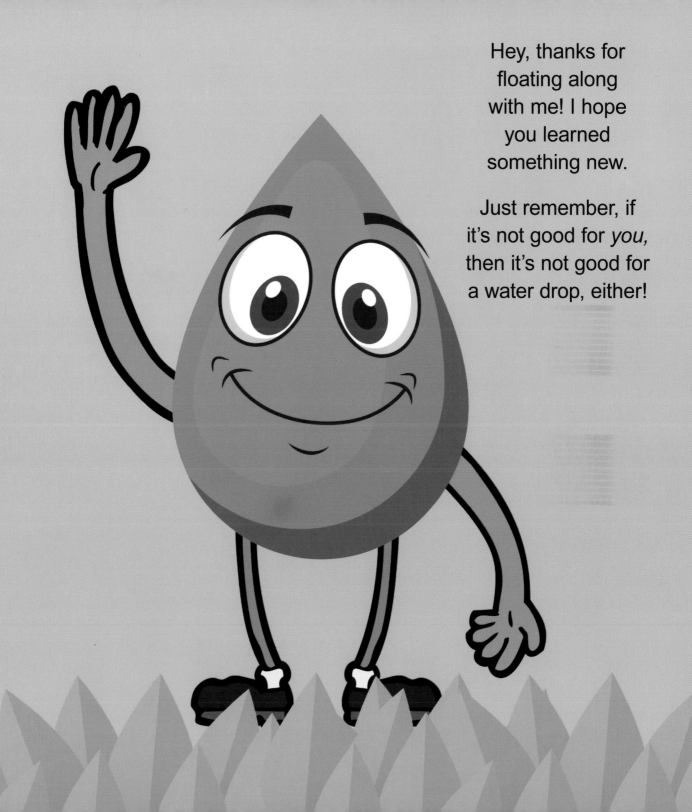

Hey, thanks for floating along with me! I hope you learned something new.

Just remember, if it's not good for *you,* then it's not good for a water drop, either!